Remembering the River...
River Runner's Journal

Logbook and Journal
For Kayakers, Rafters, Canoers,
or Any River Enthusiast

Created by:
Evolve Resource Partners, LLC
evolveresourcepartners.com
(c) 2021 Evolve Resource Partners, LLC
All rights reserved

Dedicated to Rick who has been a constant support. His love of kayaking and the joy of being on the river with friends and family have inspired the creation of this journal.

Cover Photo: Drini Teta on Unsplash
Photos: Carl Heyerdahl on Unsplash (Kayak Bow); Hu Chen on Unsplash (River at Night); Robson Hatsukami Morgan on Unsplash (Starlit River); James Fitzgerald on Unsplash (Yellowstone River); Jordan Madrid on Unsplash (Compass).

These Adventures
Belong To:

_____

> *"Thousands have lived without love, not one without water."*
> ~W.H. Auden

This logbook and journal was developed for the recreational or professional river enthusiast to document their experience of being on the river. There are prompts for the technical details of the journey, including the name of the river, river class, shuttle details, major rapids, campsites, lunch spots, hikes, and points of interest. Journal pages contain nature and river-inspired quotes with space to document highlights, inspirations, reflections, and notes from your journey. A suggested gear list is also included with blank spaces to note items to remember while packing and preparing.

Whether your trip on the river is an hour or weeks, there is plenty of room to write it all down... and help you prepare for your next adventure.

On another note...
It is imperative to protect, maintain and preserve sources of clean water. Clean flowing rivers are essential to our health, economy, and recreation. River ecosystems also provide critical habitat for fish and wildlife.

We are committed to supporting organizations that work to protect water, river access, and wildlife habitat. Please join us by visiting websites of groups such as American Whitewater, American Rivers, Waterkeeper Alliance, or similar organizations. Review the work they are doing and consider supporting or getting involved with their efforts to safeguard clean water and rivers.

Waterways require protection to preserve our ability to enjoy them, but more importantly to ensure future generations have the same opportunity.

~Enjoy the journey

Favorite Quotes
or
Words of Inspiration

_____

_____

_____

_____

_____

_____

_____

_____

_____

_____

Suggested Packing and Gear List
This list is not all inclusive, consider your individual needs
Check with your team and/or outfitter for specific list

Shared / Team Items:
- Map of area and river
- Camp toilet
- Toilet paper
- Small shovel or trowel
- Hand sanitizer
- First aid kit
- Garbage bags
- Optional: compass, binoculars, GPS communication device
- _____
- _____
- _____
- _____

Team & Individual Meal Items:
- Water bottle (with carabiner for attaching to vessel)
- Food and supplies
- Water purifier
- Utensils & cutlery
- Utility knife
- Camp bowl / plate / cup
- Stove
- Lighter / matches
- Cook set (pots)
- Biodegradable dish soap
- Dish brush and towel
- Optional:
- _____
- _____
- _____
- _____
- _____
- _____
- _____
- _____

Boating Gear:
- Vessel (kayak, raft, canoe...)
- Paddle or oar (consider spare)
- Approved personal floatation device "PFD" (life-vest)
- Whistle (attached to life-vest)
- Helmet
- Splash top
- Water shoes or sandals
- Dry bags
- Throw-bag and other river rescue equipment
- Equipment repair kit
- Knife
- Required for cold weather/water: wet suit or dry suit, insulated footwear
- _____
- _____
- _____
- _____
- _____
- _____

Menu or Other Items:
- _____
- _____
- _____
- _____
- _____
- _____
- _____
- _____
- _____
- _____
- _____
- _____

Suggested Packing and Gear List
This list is not all inclusive, consider your individual needs
Check with your team and/or outfitter for specific list

Personal Items:
- Towel – (quick-drying material)
- Biodegradable soap
- Toothbrush & toothpaste
- Bug repellant
- Medications
- Optional: lotion, facial moisturizer, deodorant, hairbrush, personal wipes, hygiene products
- _____
- _____
- _____
- _____
- _____
- _____
- _____
- _____
- _____
- _____
- _____

Clothing:
(quick-drying synthetics, not cotton)
- Bathing suit(s)
- Underwear
- Tennis shoes / hiking shoes
- Socks
- Shorts
- Short sleeve shirt (t-shirts)
- Warm / long sleeve shirt
- Warm / long pants
- Rain jacket & pants
- Warm jacket and/or fleece
- Optional: flip flops for camp, cover-up / wrap, sports bra
- _____
- _____
- _____
- _____
- _____
- _____
- _____

Sun Protection:
- Sunscreen with 30+ SPF
- Lip balm with SPF
- Sunglasses (connecting strap to prevent loss)
- Sun hat / visor
- Consider layer of protection from the sun with long sleeve tops and lightweight longer shorts / bottoms
- _____
- _____
- _____
- _____
- _____

Camp Items:
- Tent or tarp
- Sleeping bag
- Sleeping pad
- Headlamp / flashlight
- Optional: pen/pencil, book, cards inflatable pillow, camp chair
- _____
- _____
- _____
- _____
- _____
- _____
- _____
- _____

Notes...

River Log and Details

River (body of water)

_____

Section or run name...

_____

Class (1) (2) (3) (4) (5) +

Vessel (kayak, raft, canoe...)

_____

Shuttle details...

_____

_____

Put-in _____

Take-out _____

Rapids – major & notable
(name, features, rating...)

_____

_____

_____

_____

_____

Wildlife and other creatures
(bugs, fish, mammals...)

_____

_____

_____

_____

Hikes, points of interest,
excursions, fishing spots...

_____

_____

_____

_____

Date _____

Day # _____ of _____ Days

Time on _____ Time off _____

Total time _____

Distance _____

Weather and temp _____

River flow (CFS or feet) _____

Rapids portaged or
hazards to avoid...

_____

_____

_____

Who was on the trip...

_____

_____

_____

_____

Campsites & lunch spots
(or recommended next visit)...

_____

_____

_____

_____

Favorite food, drink, treat...

_____

_____

_____

_____

Day # _____ of _____ Days: Date:_____

Highlights, Quotes, Inspirations, Reflections, Notes...

_____

_____

_____

_____

_____

_____

_____

_____

_____

_____

_____

_____

_____

_____

_____

_____

_____

_____

_____

_____

"No man ever steps in the same river twice, for it's not the same river and he's not the same man."

~ Heraclitus

River Log and Details

River (body of water)
_____

Section or run name...
_____

Class ① ② ③ ④ ⑤ +

Vessel (kayak, raft, canoe...)
_____

Shuttle details...
_____
_____

Put-in _____
Take-out _____

Rapids – major & notable
(name, features, rating...)
_____
_____
_____
_____
_____
_____

Wildlife and other creatures
(bugs, fish, mammals...)
_____
_____
_____
_____

Hikes, points of interest,
excursions, fishing spots...
_____
_____
_____
_____

Date _____

Day # _____ of _____ Days

Time on _____ Time off _____

Total time _____

Distance _____

Weather and temp _____

River flow (CFS or feet) _____

Rapids portaged or
hazards to avoid...
_____
_____
_____
_____

Who was on the trip...
_____
_____
_____
_____

Campsites & lunch spots
(or recommended next visit)..
_____
_____
_____
_____

Favorite food, drink, treat...
_____
_____
_____
_____

Day # _____ of _____ Days: Date:_____

Highlights, Quotes, Inspirations, Reflections, Notes...

_____

_____

_____

_____

_____

_____

_____

_____

_____

_____

_____

_____

_____

_____

_____

_____

_____

_____

_____

"Let the mountains talk, let the river run.
Once more, and forever."

~David R. Brower

River Log and Details

River (body of water)

_____

Section or run name...

_____

Class ① ② ③ ④ ⑤ +

Vessel (kayak, raft, canoe...)

_____

Shuttle details...

_____
_____

Put-in _____
Take-out _____

Rapids – major & notable
(name, features, rating...)

_____
_____
_____
_____
_____
_____

Wildlife and other creatures
(bugs, fish, mammals...)

_____
_____
_____
_____

Hikes, points of interest,
excursions, fishing spots...

_____
_____
_____
_____

Date _____

Day # _____ of _____ Days

Time on _____ Time off _____

Total time _____

Distance _____

Weather and temp _____

River flow (CFS or feet) _____

Rapids portaged or
hazards to avoid...

_____
_____
_____
_____

Who was on the trip...

_____
_____
_____
_____

Campsites & lunch spots
(or recommended next visit)...

_____
_____
_____
_____

Favorite food, drink, treat...

_____
_____
_____
_____

Day # _____ of _____ Days: Date:_____

Highlights, Quotes, Inspirations, Reflections, Notes...

_____

_____

_____

_____

_____

_____

_____

_____

_____

_____

_____

_____

_____

_____

_____

_____

_____

_____

_____

_____

"What lies before us and what lies behind us are small matters compared to what lies within us."
~Ralph Waldo Emerson

River Log and Details

River (body of water)

_____

Section or run name...

_____

Class ① ② ③ ④ ⑤ +

Vessel (kayak, raft, canoe...)

_____

Shuttle details...

_____
_____

Put-in _____
Take-out _____

Rapids – major & notable
(name, features, rating...)

_____
_____
_____
_____
_____
_____

Wildlife and other creatures
(bugs, fish, mammals...)

_____
_____
_____
_____

Hikes, points of interest,
excursions, fishing spots...

_____
_____
_____
_____

Date _____

Day # _____ of _____ Days

Time on _____ Time off _____

Total time _____

Distance _____

Weather and temp _____

River flow (CFS or feet) _____

Rapids portaged or
hazards to avoid...

_____
_____
_____
_____

Who was on the trip...

_____
_____
_____
_____

Campsites & lunch spots
(or recommended next visit)..

_____
_____
_____
_____

Favorite food, drink, treat...

_____
_____
_____

Day # _____ of _____ Days: Date:_____

Highlights, Quotes, Inspirations, Reflections, Notes...

_____

_____

_____

_____

_____

_____

_____

_____

_____

_____

_____

_____

_____

_____

_____

_____

_____

_____

_____

"Be still like a mountain and flow like a great river."

~Lao Tse Tung

River Log and Details

River (body of water)

_____

Section or run name...

_____

Class ① ② ③ ④ ⑤ +

Vessel (kayak, raft, canoe...)

_____

Shuttle details...

_____

_____

Put-in _____

Take-out _____

Rapids – major & notable
(name, features, rating...)

_____
_____
_____
_____
_____
_____

Wildlife and other creatures
(bugs, fish, mammals...)

_____
_____
_____
_____

Hikes, points of interest,
excursions, fishing spots...

_____
_____
_____
_____

Date _____

Day # _____ of _____ Days

Time on _____ Time off _____

Total time _____

Distance _____

Weather and temp _____

River flow (CFS or feet) _____

Rapids portaged or
hazards to avoid...

_____
_____
_____

Who was on the trip...

_____
_____
_____
_____

Campsites & lunch spots
(or recommended next visit)..

_____
_____
_____
_____

Favorite food, drink, treat...

_____
_____
_____

Day # _____ of _____ Days: Date:_____

✳ Highlights, Quotes, Inspirations, Reflections, Notes...

_____

_____

_____

_____

_____

_____

_____

_____

_____

_____

_____

_____

_____

_____

_____

_____

_____

_____

> *"To put your hands in a river is to feel
> the chords that bind the earth together."*
>
> ~ Barry Lopez

River Log and Details

River (body of water)

_____

Section or run name...

_____

Class (1) (2) (3) (4) (5) +

Vessel (kayak, raft, canoe...)

_____

Shuttle details...

_____
_____

Put-in _____
Take-out _____

Rapids – major & notable
(name, features, rating...)

_____
_____
_____
_____
_____
_____

Wildlife and other creatures
(bugs, fish, mammals...)

_____
_____
_____

Hikes, points of interest,
excursions, fishing spots...

_____
_____
_____
_____

Date _____

Day # _____ of _____ Days

Time on _____ Time off _____

Total time _____

Distance _____

Weather and temp _____

River flow (CFS or feet) _____

Rapids portaged or
hazards to avoid...

_____
_____
_____
_____

Who was on the trip...

_____
_____
_____
_____

Campsites & lunch spots
(or recommended next visit)...

_____
_____
_____
_____

Favorite food, drink, treat...

_____
_____
_____
_____

Highlights, Quotes, Inspirations, Reflections, Notes...

_____

_____

_____

_____

_____

_____

_____

_____

_____

_____

_____

_____

_____

_____

_____

_____

_____

_____

"Nature is one of the most underutilized treasures in life. It has the power to unburden hearts and reconnect to that inner place of peace."
~ Janice Anderson

River Log and Details

River (body of water)

_____

Section or run name...

_____

Class ① ② ③ ④ ⑤ +

Vessel (kayak, raft, canoe...)

_____

Shuttle details...

_____
_____

Put-in _____
Take-out _____

Rapids – major & notable
(name, features, rating...)

_____
_____
_____
_____
_____
_____

Wildlife and other creatures
(bugs, fish, mammals...)

_____
_____
_____
_____

Hikes, points of interest,
excursions, fishing spots...

_____
_____
_____
_____

Date _____

Day # _____ of _____ Days

Time on _____ Time off _____

Total time _____

Distance _____

Weather and temp _____

River flow (CFS or feet) _____

Rapids portaged or
hazards to avoid...

_____
_____
_____
_____

Who was on the trip...

_____
_____
_____
_____

Campsites & lunch spots
(or recommended next visit)...

_____
_____
_____
_____

Favorite food, drink, treat...

_____
_____
_____
_____

© Evolve Resource Partners, LLC

Day # _____ of _____ Days: Date:_____

✦ Highlights, Quotes, Inspirations, Reflections, Notes...

_____

_____

_____

_____

_____

_____

_____

_____

_____

_____

_____

_____

_____

_____

_____

_____

_____

_____

_____

"My favourite places on earth are the wild waterways
where the forest opens its arms and a silver curve of
river folds the traveller into its embrace."
~Rory MacLean

River Log and Details

River (body of water)

_____

Section or run name...

_____

Class ① ② ③ ④ ⑤ +

Vessel (kayak, raft, canoe...)

_____

Shuttle details...

_____

_____

Put-in _____

Take-out _____

Rapids – major & notable
(name, features, rating...)

_____
_____
_____
_____
_____

Wildlife and other creatures
(bugs, fish, mammals...)

_____
_____
_____
_____

Hikes, points of interest,
excursions, fishing spots...

_____
_____
_____
_____

Date _____

Day # _____ of _____ Days

Time on _____ Time off _____

Total time _____

Distance _____

Weather and temp _____

River flow (CFS or feet) _____

Rapids portaged or
hazards to avoid...

_____
_____
_____
_____

Who was on the trip...

_____
_____
_____
_____

Campsites & lunch spots
(or recommended next visit)...

_____
_____
_____
_____

Favorite food, drink, treat...

_____
_____
_____
_____

Highlights, Quotes, Inspirations, Reflections, Notes...

_____

_____

_____

_____

_____

_____

_____

_____

_____

_____

_____

_____

_____

_____

_____

_____

_____

_____

"Eventually, all things merge into one,
and a river runs through it."

~Norman Maclean

River Log and Details

River (body of water)

_____

Section or run name...

_____

Class (1) (2) (3) (4) (5) +

Vessel (kayak, raft, canoe...)

_____

Shuttle details...

_____
_____

Put-in _____
Take-out _____

Rapids – major & notable
(name, features, rating...)

_____
_____
_____
_____
_____
_____

Wildlife and other creatures
(bugs, fish, mammals...)

_____
_____
_____
_____

Hikes, points of interest,
excursions, fishing spots...

_____
_____
_____
_____
_____

Date _____

Day # _____ of _____ Days

Time on _____ Time off _____

Total time _____

Distance _____

Weather and temp _____

River flow (CFS or feet) _____

Rapids portaged or
hazards to avoid...

_____
_____
_____
_____

Who was on the trip...

_____
_____
_____
_____

Campsites & lunch spots
(or recommended next visit)...

_____
_____
_____
_____

Favorite food, drink, treat...

_____
_____
_____
_____

Highlights, Quotes, Inspirations, Reflections, Notes...

_____

_____

_____

_____

_____

_____

_____

_____

_____

_____

_____

_____

_____

_____

_____

_____

_____

_____

_____

"There's more to life than speeding it up."

~ Gandhi

River Log and Details

River (body of water)

_____

Section or run name...

_____

Class ① ② ③ ④ ⑤ +

Vessel (kayak, raft, canoe...)

_____

Shuttle details...

_____
_____

Put-in _____

Take-out _____

Rapids – major & notable (name, features, rating...)

_____
_____
_____
_____
_____
_____

Wildlife and other creatures (bugs, fish, mammals...)

_____
_____
_____
_____

Hikes, points of interest, excursions, fishing spots...

_____
_____
_____
_____

Date _____

Day # _____ of _____ Days

Time on _____ Time off _____

Total time _____

Distance _____

Weather and temp _____

River flow (CFS or feet) _____

Rapids portaged or hazards to avoid...

_____
_____
_____
_____

Who was on the trip...

_____
_____
_____
_____

Campsites & lunch spots (or recommended next visit)..

_____
_____
_____
_____

Favorite food, drink, treat...

_____
_____
_____
_____

Day # _____ of _____ Days: Date:_____

Highlights, Quotes, Inspirations, Reflections, Notes...

_____

_____

_____

_____

_____

_____

_____

_____

_____

_____

_____

_____

_____

_____

_____

_____

_____

_____

_____

*"Life sometimes takes you into troubled waters
not to drown you but to cleanse you."*

~Unknown

River Log and Details

River (body of water)
_____

Section or run name...
_____

Class ① ② ③ ④ ⑤ +

Vessel (kayak, raft, canoe...)
_____

Shuttle details...
_____
_____

Put-in _____
Take-out _____

Rapids – major & notable
(name, features, rating...)
_____
_____
_____
_____
_____
_____

Wildlife and other creatures
(bugs, fish, mammals...)
_____
_____
_____
_____

Hikes, points of interest,
excursions, fishing spots...
_____
_____
_____
_____

Date _____

Day # _____ of _____ Days

Time on _____ Time off _____

Total time _____

Distance _____

Weather and temp _____

River flow (CFS or feet) _____

Rapids portaged or
hazards to avoid...
_____
_____
_____
_____

Who was on the trip...
_____
_____
_____
_____

Campsites & lunch spots
(or recommended next visit)...
_____
_____
_____
_____

Favorite food, drink, treat...
_____
_____
_____
_____

Highlights, Quotes, Inspirations, Reflections, Notes...

_____

_____

_____

_____

_____

_____

_____

_____

_____

_____

_____

_____

_____

_____

_____

_____

_____

_____

_____

_____

"Real freedom lies in wildness, not in civilization."
~Charles Lindbergh

River Log and Details

River (body of water)
_____
Section or run name...

_____

Class ① ② ③ ④ ⑤ +

Vessel (kayak, raft, canoe...)
_____

Shuttle details...
_____
_____

Put-in _____
Take-out _____

Rapids – major & notable
(name, features, rating...)
_____
_____
_____
_____
_____
_____

Wildlife and other creatures
(bugs, fish, mammals...)
_____
_____
_____
_____

Hikes, points of interest,
excursions, fishing spots...
_____
_____
_____
_____

Date _____

Day # _____ of _____ Days

Time on _____ Time off _____

Total time _____

Distance _____

Weather and temp _____

River flow (CFS or feet) _____

Rapids portaged or
hazards to avoid...
_____
_____
_____
_____

Who was on the trip...
_____
_____
_____
_____

Campsites & lunch spots
(or recommended next visit)...
_____
_____
_____
_____

Favorite food, drink, treat...
_____
_____
_____
_____

© Evolve Resource Partners, LLC

Day # _____ of _____ Days: Date:_____

Highlights, Quotes, Inspirations, Reflections, Notes...

_____

_____

_____

_____

_____

_____

_____

_____

_____

_____

_____

_____

_____

_____

_____

_____

_____

_____

"Wilderness is not a luxury but a necessity of the
human spirit, and as vital to our lives
as water and good bread."
~Edward Abbey

River Log and Details

River (body of water)

_____

Section or run name...

_____

Class ① ② ③ ④ ⑤ +

Vessel (kayak, raft, canoe...)

_____

Shuttle details...

_____
_____

Put-in _____
Take-out _____

Rapids – major & notable
(name, features, rating...)

_____
_____
_____
_____
_____
_____

Wildlife and other creatures
(bugs, fish, mammals...)

_____
_____
_____
_____

Hikes, points of interest,
excursions, fishing spots...

_____
_____
_____
_____
_____

Date _____

Day # _____ of _____ Days

Time on _____ Time off _____

Total time _____

Distance _____

Weather and temp _____

River flow (CFS or feet) _____

Rapids portaged or
hazards to avoid...

_____
_____
_____
_____

Who was on the trip...

_____
_____
_____
_____

Campsites & lunch spots
(or recommended next visit)...

_____
_____
_____
_____

Favorite food, drink, treat...

_____
_____
_____

Day # _____ of _____ Days: Date:_____

Highlights, Quotes, Inspirations, Reflections, Notes...

_____

_____

_____

_____

_____

_____

_____

_____

_____

_____

_____

_____

_____

_____

_____

_____

_____

_____

"The sun shines not on us but in us.
The rivers flow not past, but through us."

~John Muir

River Log and Details

River (body of water)
_____

Section or run name...
_____

Class ① ② ③ ④ ⑤ +

Vessel (kayak, raft, canoe...)
_____

Shuttle details...
_____
_____

Put-in _____
Take-out _____

Rapids – major & notable
(name, features, rating...)
_____
_____
_____
_____
_____
_____

Wildlife and other creatures
(bugs, fish, mammals...)
_____
_____
_____
_____

Hikes, points of interest,
excursions, fishing spots...
_____
_____
_____
_____

Date _____

Day # _____ of _____ Days

Time on _____ Time off _____

Total time _____

Distance _____

Weather and temp _____

River flow (CFS or feet) _____

Rapids portaged or
hazards to avoid...
_____
_____
_____
_____

Who was on the trip...
_____
_____
_____
_____

Campsites & lunch spots
(or recommended next visit)..
_____
_____
_____
_____

Favorite food, drink, treat...
_____
_____
_____
_____

Highlights, Quotes, Inspirations, Reflections, Notes...

_____

_____

_____

_____

_____

_____

_____

_____

_____

_____

_____

_____

_____

_____

_____

_____

"For life and death are one,
even as the river and the sea are one."

~Khalil Gibran

River Log and Details

River (body of water)

_____

Section or run name...

_____

Class (1) (2) (3) (4) (5) +

Vessel (kayak, raft, canoe...)

_____

Shuttle details...

_____

_____

Put-in _____

Take-out _____

Rapids – major & notable
(name, features, rating...)

_____
_____
_____
_____
_____
_____

Wildlife and other creatures
(bugs, fish, mammals...)

_____
_____
_____
_____

Hikes, points of interest,
excursions, fishing spots...

_____
_____
_____
_____

Date _____

Day # _____ of _____ Days

Time on _____ Time off _____

Total time _____

Distance _____

Weather and temp _____

River flow (CFS or feet) _____

Rapids portaged or
hazards to avoid...

_____
_____
_____
_____

Who was on the trip...

_____
_____
_____
_____

Campsites & lunch spots
(or recommended next visit)...

_____
_____
_____
_____

Favorite food, drink, treat...

_____
_____
_____
_____

Highlights, Quotes, Inspirations, Reflections, Notes...

_____

_____

_____

_____

_____

_____

_____

_____

_____

_____

_____

_____

_____

_____

_____

_____

_____

_____

"Not all those who wander are lost."

~J.R.R. Tolkien

River Log and Details

River (body of water)

_____

Section or run name…

_____

Class ① ② ③ ④ ⑤ +

Vessel (kayak, raft, canoe…)

_____

Shuttle details…

_____
_____

Put-in _____
Take-out _____

Rapids – major & notable
(name, features, rating…)

_____
_____
_____
_____
_____
_____

Wildlife and other creatures
(bugs, fish, mammals…)

_____
_____
_____
_____

Hikes, points of interest,
excursions, fishing spots…

_____
_____
_____
_____

Date _____

Day # _____ of _____ Days

Time on _____ Time off _____

Total time _____

Distance _____

Weather and temp _____

River flow (CFS or feet) _____

Rapids portaged or
hazards to avoid…

_____
_____
_____
_____

Who was on the trip…

_____
_____
_____
_____

Campsites & lunch spots
(or recommended next visit)…

_____
_____
_____
_____

Favorite food, drink, treat…

_____
_____
_____
_____

Day # _____ of _____ Days: Date:_____

✦ Highlights, Quotes, Inspirations, Reflections, Notes...

_____

_____

_____

_____

_____

_____

_____

_____

_____

_____

_____

_____

_____

_____

_____

_____

_____

_____

*"For after all, the best thing one can do
when it is raining, is to let it rain."*

~Henry Wadsworth Longfellow

River Log and Details

River (body of water)
_____

Section or run name...
_____

Class ① ② ③ ④ ⑤ +

Vessel (kayak, raft, canoe...)
_____

Shuttle details...
_____
_____

Put-in _____
Take-out _____

Rapids – major & notable
(name, features, rating...)
_____
_____
_____
_____
_____
_____

Wildlife and other creatures
(bugs, fish, mammals...)
_____
_____
_____
_____

Hikes, points of interest,
excursions, fishing spots...
_____
_____
_____
_____

Date _____

Day # _____ of _____ Days

Time on _____ Time off _____

Total time _____

Distance _____

Weather and temp _____

River flow (CFS or feet) _____

Rapids portaged or
hazards to avoid...
_____
_____
_____
_____

Who was on the trip...
_____
_____
_____
_____

Campsites & lunch spots
(or recommended next visit)..
_____
_____
_____
_____

Favorite food, drink, treat...
_____
_____
_____
_____

Day # _____ of _____ Days: Date:_____

Highlights, Quotes, Inspirations, Reflections, Notes...

_____

_____

_____

_____

_____

_____

_____

_____

_____

_____

_____

_____

_____

_____

_____

_____

_____

_____

"Rivers are places that renew our spirit,
connect us with our past, and link us directly with the
flow and rhythm of the natural world."
~Ted Turner

River Log and Details

River (body of water)

_____

Section or run name...

_____

Class (1) (2) (3) (4) (5) +

Vessel (kayak, raft, canoe...)

_____

Shuttle details...

_____
_____

Put-in _____
Take-out _____

Rapids – major & notable
(name, features, rating...)

_____
_____
_____
_____
_____
_____

Wildlife and other creatures
(bugs, fish, mammals...)

_____
_____
_____
_____

Hikes, points of interest,
excursions, fishing spots...

_____
_____
_____
_____
_____

Date _____

Day # _____ of _____ Days

Time on _____ Time off _____

Total time _____

Distance _____

Weather and temp _____

River flow (CFS or feet) _____

Rapids portaged or
hazards to avoid...

_____
_____
_____
_____

Who was on the trip...

_____
_____
_____
_____

Campsites & lunch spots
(or recommended next visit)...

_____
_____
_____
_____

Favorite food, drink, treat...

_____
_____
_____
_____

Day # _____ of _____ Days: Date:_____

Highlights, Quotes, Inspirations, Reflections, Notes...

_____

_____

_____

_____

_____

_____

_____

_____

_____

_____

_____

_____

_____

_____

_____

_____

_____

_____

_____

_____

"Rivers know this: there is no hurry.
We shall get there someday."

~A. A. Milne

River Log and Details

River (body of water)

_____

Section or run name...

_____

Class ① ② ③ ④ ⑤ +

Vessel (kayak, raft, canoe...)

_____

Shuttle details...

_____
_____

Put-in _____
Take-out _____

Rapids – major & notable
(name, features, rating...)

_____
_____
_____
_____
_____
_____

Wildlife and other creatures
(bugs, fish, mammals...)

_____
_____
_____
_____

Hikes, points of interest,
excursions, fishing spots...

_____
_____
_____
_____

Date _____

Day # _____ of _____ Days

Time on _____ Time off _____

Total time _____

Distance _____

Weather and temp _____

River flow (CFS or feet) _____

Rapids portaged or
hazards to avoid...

_____
_____
_____
_____

Who was on the trip...

_____
_____
_____
_____

Campsites & lunch spots
(or recommended next visit)..

_____
_____
_____
_____

Favorite food, drink, treat...

_____
_____
_____
_____

Day # _____ of _____ Days: Date:_____

Highlights, Quotes, Inspirations, Reflections, Notes...

_____

_____

_____

_____

_____

_____

_____

_____

_____

_____

_____

_____

_____

_____

_____

_____

_____

_____

_____

"One touch of nature makes the whole world kin."

~William Shakespeare

River Log and Details

River (body of water)
_____

Section or run name...

_____

Class (1) (2) (3) (4) (5) +

Vessel (kayak, raft, canoe...)

_____

Shuttle details...

_____
_____

Put-in _____
Take-out _____

Rapids – major & notable
(name, features, rating...)

_____
_____
_____
_____
_____
_____

Wildlife and other creatures
(bugs, fish, mammals...)

_____
_____
_____
_____

Hikes, points of interest,
excursions, fishing spots...

_____
_____
_____
_____

Date _____

Day # _____ of _____ Days

Time on _____ Time off _____

Total time _____

Distance _____

Weather and temp _____

River flow (CFS or feet) _____

Rapids portaged or
hazards to avoid...

_____
_____
_____
_____

Who was on the trip...

_____
_____
_____
_____

Campsites & lunch spots
(or recommended next visit)...

_____
_____
_____
_____

Favorite food, drink, treat...

_____
_____
_____
_____

Highlights, Quotes, Inspirations, Reflections, Notes...

_____

_____

_____

_____

_____

_____

_____

_____

_____

_____

_____

_____

_____

_____

_____

_____

_____

"Sometimes luck is with you, and sometimes not, but the important thing is to take the dare. Those who climb mountains or raft rivers understand this."
~David R. Brower

River Log and Details

River (body of water)

_____

Section or run name...

_____

Class (1) (2) (3) (4) (5) +

Vessel (kayak, raft, canoe...)

_____

Shuttle details...

_____
_____

Put-in _____
Take-out _____

Rapids – major & notable
(name, features, rating...)

_____
_____
_____
_____
_____
_____

Wildlife and other creatures
(bugs, fish, mammals...)

_____
_____
_____
_____

Hikes, points of interest,
excursions, fishing spots...

_____
_____
_____
_____

Date _____

Day # _____ of _____ Days

Time on _____ Time off _____

Total time _____

Distance _____

Weather and temp _____

River flow (CFS or feet) _____

Rapids portaged or
hazards to avoid...

_____
_____
_____
_____

Who was on the trip...

_____
_____
_____
_____

Campsites & lunch spots
(or recommended next visit)...

_____
_____
_____
_____

Favorite food, drink, treat...

_____
_____
_____
_____

Day # _____ of _____ Days: Date:_____

Highlights, Quotes, Inspirations, Reflections, Notes...

_____

_____

_____

_____

_____

_____

_____

_____

_____

_____

_____

_____

_____

_____

_____

_____

_____

_____

_____

"You can't be unhappy in the middle of a big, beautiful river."

~Jim Harrison

River Log and Details

River (body of water)
_____

Section or run name...
_____

Class (1) (2) (3) (4) (5) +

Vessel (kayak, raft, canoe...)
_____

Shuttle details...
_____
_____

Put-in _____
Take-out _____

Rapids – major & notable
(name, features, rating...)
_____
_____
_____
_____
_____
_____

Wildlife and other creatures
(bugs, fish, mammals...)
_____
_____
_____
_____

Hikes, points of interest,
excursions, fishing spots...
_____
_____
_____
_____

Date _____

Day # _____ of _____ Days

Time on _____ Time off _____

Total time _____

Distance _____

Weather and temp _____

River flow (CFS or feet) _____

Rapids portaged or
hazards to avoid...
_____
_____
_____
_____

Who was on the trip...
_____
_____
_____
_____

Campsites & lunch spots
(or recommended next visit)..
_____
_____
_____
_____

Favorite food, drink, treat...
_____
_____
_____
_____

Day # _____ of _____ Days: Date:_____

Highlights, Quotes, Inspirations, Reflections, Notes...

_____

_____

_____

_____

_____

_____

_____

_____

_____

_____

_____

_____

_____

_____

_____

_____

_____

_____

_____

_____

_____

"Live the life you've dreamed."

~Henry David Thoreau

River Log and Details

River (body of water)

_____

Section or run name...

_____

Class ① ② ③ ④ ⑤ +

Vessel (kayak, raft, canoe...)

_____

Shuttle details...

_____
_____

Put-in _____

Take-out _____

Rapids – major & notable
(name, features, rating...)

_____
_____
_____
_____
_____
_____

Wildlife and other creatures
(bugs, fish, mammals...)

_____
_____
_____
_____

Hikes, points of interest,
excursions, fishing spots...

_____
_____
_____
_____

Date _____

Day # _____ of _____ Days

Time on _____ Time off _____

Total time _____

Distance _____

Weather and temp _____

River flow (CFS or feet) _____

Rapids portaged or
hazards to avoid...

_____
_____
_____
_____

Who was on the trip...

_____
_____
_____
_____

Campsites & lunch spots
(or recommended next visit)...

_____
_____
_____
_____

Favorite food, drink, treat...

_____
_____
_____
_____

Highlights, Quotes, Inspirations, Reflections, Notes...

_____

_____

_____

_____

_____

_____

_____

_____

_____

_____

_____

_____

_____

_____

_____

_____

_____

"Change not the river, for rocks in the river are good and are like our problems – without them we would not know if there was any current."

~Dennis Mapes

River Log and Details

River (body of water)

_____

Section or run name...

_____

Class (1) (2) (3) (4) (5) +

Vessel (kayak, raft, canoe...)

_____

Shuttle details...

_____
_____

Put-in _____
Take-out _____

Rapids – major & notable
(name, features, rating...)

_____
_____
_____
_____
_____
_____

Wildlife and other creatures
(bugs, fish, mammals...)

_____
_____
_____
_____

Hikes, points of interest,
excursions, fishing spots...

_____
_____
_____
_____

Date _____

Day # _____ of _____ Days

Time on _____ Time off _____

Total time _____

Distance _____

Weather and temp _____

River flow (CFS or feet) _____

Rapids portaged or
hazards to avoid...

_____
_____
_____
_____

Who was on the trip...

_____
_____
_____
_____

Campsites & lunch spots
(or recommended next visit)...

_____
_____
_____
_____

Favorite food, drink, treat...

_____
_____
_____
_____

Day # _____ of _____ Days: Date:_____

Highlights, Quotes, Inspirations, Reflections, Notes...

_____

_____

_____

_____

_____

_____

_____

_____

_____

_____

_____

_____

_____

_____

_____

_____

_____

_____

*"May your choices reflect your hopes
not your fears."*

~Nelson Mandela

River Log and Details

River (body of water)
_____

Section or run name...
_____

Class (1) (2) (3) (4) (5) +

Vessel (kayak, raft, canoe...)
_____

Shuttle details...
_____
_____

Put-in _____
Take-out _____

Rapids – major & notable
(name, features, rating...)
_____
_____
_____
_____
_____
_____

Wildlife and other creatures
(bugs, fish, mammals...)
_____
_____
_____
_____

Hikes, points of interest,
excursions, fishing spots...
_____
_____
_____
_____
_____

Date _____

Day # _____ of _____ Days

Time on _____ Time off _____

Total time _____

Distance _____

Weather and temp _____

River flow (CFS or feet) _____

Rapids portaged or
hazards to avoid...
_____
_____
_____
_____

Who was on the trip...
_____
_____
_____
_____

Campsites & lunch spots
(or recommended next visit)..
_____
_____
_____
_____

Favorite food, drink, treat...
_____
_____
_____

Day # _____ of _____ Days: Date:_____

Highlights, Quotes, Inspirations, Reflections, Notes...

_____

_____

_____

_____

_____

_____

_____

_____

_____

_____

_____

_____

_____

_____

_____

_____

_____

_____

"The first river you paddle runs through the rest of your life. It bubbles up in pools and eddies to remind you who you are."

~Lynn Noel

River Log and Details

River (body of water)

_____

Section or run name...

_____

Class (1) (2) (3) (4) (5) +

Vessel (kayak, raft, canoe...)

_____

Shuttle details...

_____

_____

Put-in _____

Take-out _____

Rapids – major & notable (name, features, rating...)

_____
_____
_____
_____
_____

Wildlife and other creatures (bugs, fish, mammals...)

_____
_____
_____
_____

Hikes, points of interest, excursions, fishing spots...

_____
_____
_____
_____

Date _____

Day # _____ of _____ Days

Time on _____ Time off _____

Total time _____

Distance _____

Weather and temp _____

River flow (CFS or feet) _____

Rapids portaged or hazards to avoid...

_____
_____
_____
_____

Who was on the trip...

_____
_____
_____
_____

Campsites & lunch spots (or recommended next visit)..

_____
_____
_____
_____

Favorite food, drink, treat...

_____
_____
_____

Day # _____ of _____ Days: Date:_____

✦ Highlights, Quotes, Inspirations, Reflections, Notes...

_____

_____

_____

_____

_____

_____

_____

_____

_____

_____

_____

_____

_____

_____

_____

_____

_____

_____

"Reaction – a boat which is going against the current, but which does not prevent the river from flowing on."

~Victor Hugo

River Log and Details

River (body of water)
_____

Section or run name…
_____

Class ① ② ③ ④ ⑤ +

Vessel (kayak, raft, canoe…)
_____

Shuttle details…
_____
_____

Put-in _____
Take-out _____

Rapids – major & notable
(name, features, rating…)
_____
_____
_____
_____
_____
_____

Wildlife and other creatures
(bugs, fish, mammals…)
_____
_____
_____
_____

Hikes, points of interest,
excursions, fishing spots…
_____
_____
_____
_____
_____

Date _____

Day # _____ of _____ Days

Time on _____ Time off _____

Total time _____

Distance _____

Weather and temp _____

River flow (CFS or feet) _____

Rapids portaged or
hazards to avoid…
_____
_____
_____
_____

Who was on the trip…
_____
_____
_____
_____

Campsites & lunch spots
(or recommended next visit)..
_____
_____
_____
_____

Favorite food, drink, treat…
_____
_____
_____
_____

Day # _____ of _____ Days: Date:_____

Highlights, Quotes, Inspirations, Reflections, Notes...

_____

_____

_____

_____

_____

_____

_____

_____

_____

_____

_____

_____

_____

_____

_____

_____

_____

_____

"Nothing is softer or more flexible than water,
yet nothing can resist it."

~Lao Tzu

River Log and Details

River (body of water)

_____

Section or run name...

_____

Class (1) (2) (3) (4) (5) +

Vessel (kayak, raft, canoe...)

_____

Shuttle details...

_____
_____

Put-in _____
Take-out _____

Rapids – major & notable
(name, features, rating...)

_____
_____
_____
_____
_____
_____

Wildlife and other creatures
(bugs, fish, mammals...)

_____
_____
_____
_____

Hikes, points of interest,
excursions, fishing spots...

_____
_____
_____
_____
_____

Date _____

Day # _____ of _____ Days

Time on _____ Time off _____

Total time _____

Distance _____

Weather and temp _____

River flow (CFS or feet) _____

Rapids portaged or
hazards to avoid...

_____
_____
_____
_____

Who was on the trip...

_____
_____
_____
_____

Campsites & lunch spots
(or recommended next visit)..

_____
_____
_____
_____

Favorite food, drink, treat...

_____
_____
_____
_____

Day # _____ of _____ Days: Date:_____

Highlights, Quotes, Inspirations, Reflections, Notes...

_____

_____

_____

_____

_____

_____

_____

_____

_____

_____

_____

_____

_____

_____

_____

_____

_____

_____

_____

_____

"When the well's dry, we know the worth of water."
~Benjamin Franklin

River Log and Details

River (body of water)

_____

Section or run name...

_____

Class ① ② ③ ④ ⑤ +

Vessel (kayak, raft, canoe...)

_____

Shuttle details...

_____
_____

Put-in _____
Take-out _____

Rapids – major & notable (name, features, rating...)

_____
_____
_____
_____
_____
_____

Wildlife and other creatures (bugs, fish, mammals...)

_____
_____
_____
_____

Hikes, points of interest, excursions, fishing spots...

_____
_____
_____
_____

Date _____

Day # _____ of _____ Days

Time on _____ Time off _____

Total time _____

Distance _____

Weather and temp _____

River flow (CFS or feet) _____

Rapids portaged or hazards to avoid...

_____
_____
_____
_____

Who was on the trip...

_____
_____
_____
_____

Campsites & lunch spots (or recommended next visit)...

_____
_____
_____
_____

Favorite food, drink, treat...

_____
_____
_____
_____

Day # _____ of _____ Days: Date:_____

Highlights, Quotes, Inspirations, Reflections, Notes...

_____

_____

_____

_____

_____

_____

_____

_____

_____

_____

_____

_____

_____

_____

_____

_____

_____

_____

*"Many a calm river begins as a turbulent waterfall,
yet none hurtles and foams all the way to the sea."*

~Mikhail Lermontov

River Log and Details

River (body of water)

_____

Section or run name...

_____

Class (1) (2) (3) (4) (5) +

Vessel (kayak, raft, canoe...)

_____

Shuttle details...

_____
_____

Put-in _____

Take-out _____

Rapids – major & notable
(name, features, rating...)

_____
_____
_____
_____
_____
_____

Wildlife and other creatures
(bugs, fish, mammals...)

_____
_____
_____
_____

Hikes, points of interest,
excursions, fishing spots...

_____
_____
_____
_____

Date _____

Day # _____ of _____ Days

Time on _____ Time off _____

Total time _____

Distance _____

Weather and temp _____

River flow (CFS or feet) _____

Rapids portaged or
hazards to avoid...

_____
_____
_____
_____

Who was on the trip...

_____
_____
_____
_____

Campsites & lunch spots
(or recommended next visit)...

_____
_____
_____
_____

Favorite food, drink, treat...

_____
_____
_____
_____

Day # _____ of _____ Days: Date:_____

Highlights, Quotes, Inspirations, Reflections, Notes...

_____

_____

_____

_____

_____

_____

_____

_____

_____

_____

_____

_____

_____

_____

_____

_____

_____

_____

_____

"What makes a river so restful to people is that it doesn't have any doubt – it is sure to get where it is going, and it doesn't want to go anywhere else."
                                                              ~Hal Boyle

River Log and Details

River (body of water)

_____
Section or run name...

_____

Class ① ② ③ ④ ⑤ +

Vessel (kayak, raft, canoe...)

_____

Shuttle details...

_____
_____

Put-in _____
Take-out _____

Rapids – major & notable
(name, features, rating...)

_____
_____
_____
_____
_____
_____

Wildlife and other creatures
(bugs, fish, mammals...)

_____
_____
_____
_____

Hikes, points of interest,
excursions, fishing spots...

_____
_____
_____
_____

Date _____

Day # _____ of _____ Days

Time on _____ Time off _____

Total time _____

Distance _____

Weather and temp _____

River flow (CFS or feet) _____

Rapids portaged or
hazards to avoid...

_____
_____
_____
_____

Who was on the trip...

_____
_____
_____
_____

Campsites & lunch spots
(or recommended next visit)..

_____
_____
_____
_____

Favorite food, drink, treat...

_____
_____
_____
_____

Highlights, Quotes, Inspirations, Reflections, Notes...

_____

_____

_____

_____

_____

_____

_____

_____

_____

_____

_____

_____

_____

_____

_____

_____

"A river is more than an amenity...it is a treasure. It offers a necessity of life that must be rationed among those who have power over it."

~Oliver Wendell Holmes, Jr.

River Log and Details

River (body of water)
_____

Section or run name...
_____

Class (1) (2) (3) (4) (5) +

Vessel (kayak, raft, canoe...)
_____

Shuttle details...
_____
_____

Put-in _____
Take-out _____

Rapids – major & notable
(name, features, rating...)
_____
_____
_____
_____
_____
_____

Wildlife and other creatures
(bugs, fish, mammals...)
_____
_____
_____
_____

Hikes, points of interest,
excursions, fishing spots...
_____
_____
_____
_____

Date _____

Day # _____ of _____ Days

Time on _____ Time off _____

Total time _____

Distance _____

Weather and temp _____

River flow (CFS or feet) _____

Rapids portaged or
hazards to avoid...
_____
_____
_____
_____

Who was on the trip...
_____
_____
_____
_____

Campsites & lunch spots
(or recommended next visit)...
_____
_____
_____
_____

Favorite food, drink, treat...
_____
_____
_____

Day # _____ of _____ Days: Date:_____

✦ Highlights, Quotes, Inspirations, Reflections, Notes...

_____

_____

_____

_____

_____

_____

_____

_____

_____

_____

_____

_____

_____

_____

_____

_____

_____

_____

"Earth and Sky, Woods and Fields, Lakes and Rivers, the Mountain and the Sea, are excellent schoolmasters, and teach some of us more than we can ever learn from books."
~John Lubbock

River Log and Details

River (body of water)

_____

Section or run name...

_____

Class ① ② ③ ④ ⑤ +

Vessel (kayak, raft, canoe...)

_____

Shuttle details...

_____
_____

Put-in _____
Take-out _____

Rapids – major & notable
(name, features, rating...)

_____
_____
_____
_____
_____
_____

Wildlife and other creatures
(bugs, fish, mammals...)

_____
_____
_____
_____

Hikes, points of interest,
excursions, fishing spots...

_____
_____
_____
_____

Date _____

Day # _____ of _____ Days

Time on _____ Time off _____

Total time _____

Distance _____

Weather and temp _____

River flow (CFS or feet) _____

Rapids portaged or
hazards to avoid...

_____
_____
_____
_____

Who was on the trip...

_____
_____
_____
_____

Campsites & lunch spots
(or recommended next visit)..

_____
_____
_____
_____

Favorite food, drink, treat...

_____
_____
_____
_____

Day # _____ of _____ Days: Date:_____

Highlights, Quotes, Inspirations, Reflections, Notes...

_____

_____

_____

_____

_____

_____

_____

_____

_____

_____

_____

_____

_____

_____

_____

_____

_____

> *"In all things of nature*
> *there is something of the marvelous."*
>
> ~Aristotle

River Log and Details

River (body of water)

_____

Section or run name…

_____

Class ① ② ③ ④ ⑤ +

Vessel (kayak, raft, canoe…)

_____

Shuttle details…

_____
_____

Put-in _____
Take-out _____

Rapids – major & notable
(name, features, rating…)

_____
_____
_____
_____
_____
_____

Wildlife and other creatures
(bugs, fish, mammals…)

_____
_____
_____
_____

Hikes, points of interest,
excursions, fishing spots…

_____
_____
_____
_____

Date _____

Day # _____ of _____ Days

Time on _____ Time off _____

Total time _____

Distance _____

Weather and temp _____

River flow (CFS or feet) _____

Rapids portaged or
hazards to avoid…

_____
_____
_____
_____

Who was on the trip…

_____
_____
_____
_____

Campsites & lunch spots
(or recommended next visit)…

_____
_____
_____
_____

Favorite food, drink, treat…

_____
_____
_____
_____

Day # _____ of _____ Days: Date:_____

Highlights, Quotes, Inspirations, Reflections, Notes...

_____

_____

_____

_____

_____

_____

_____

_____

_____

_____

_____

_____

_____

_____

_____

_____

_____

_____

_____

_____

"I see an America whose rivers and valleys and lakes, hills and streams and plains, the mountains over our land and nature's wealth deep under the earth, are protected as the rightful heritage of all the people." ~Franklin D. Roosevelt

River Log and Details

River (body of water)

_____

Section or run name...

_____

Class ① ② ③ ④ ⑤ +

Vessel (kayak, raft, canoe...)

_____

Shuttle details...

_____

_____

Put-in _____
Take-out _____

Rapids – major & notable
(name, features, rating...)

_____
_____
_____
_____
_____

Wildlife and other creatures
(bugs, fish, mammals...)

_____
_____
_____
_____

Hikes, points of interest,
excursions, fishing spots...

_____
_____
_____
_____

Date _____

Day # _____ of _____ Days

Time on _____ Time off _____

Total time _____

Distance _____

Weather and temp _____

River flow (CFS or feet) _____

Rapids portaged or
hazards to avoid...

_____
_____
_____

Who was on the trip...

_____
_____
_____
_____

Campsites & lunch spots
(or recommended next visit)...

_____
_____
_____
_____

Favorite food, drink, treat...

_____
_____
_____

Highlights, Quotes, Inspirations, Reflections, Notes...

_____

_____

_____

_____

_____

_____

_____

_____

_____

_____

_____

_____

_____

_____

_____

_____

_____

"If one truly loves nature one finds beauty everywhere."
~Vincent Van Gogh

River Log and Details

River (body of water)

_____

Section or run name...

_____

Class (1) (2) (3) (4) (5) +

Vessel (kayak, raft, canoe...)

_____

Shuttle details...

_____
_____

Put-in _____
Take-out _____

Rapids – major & notable
(name, features, rating...)

_____
_____
_____
_____
_____
_____

Wildlife and other creatures
(bugs, fish, mammals...)

_____
_____
_____
_____

Hikes, points of interest,
excursions, fishing spots...

_____
_____
_____
_____

Date _____

Day # _____ of _____ Days

Time on _____ Time off _____

Total time _____

Distance _____

Weather and temp _____

River flow (CFS or feet) _____

Rapids portaged or
hazards to avoid...

_____
_____
_____
_____

Who was on the trip...

_____
_____
_____
_____

Campsites & lunch spots
(or recommended next visit)..

_____
_____
_____
_____

Favorite food, drink, treat...

_____
_____
_____
_____

Day # _____ of _____ Days: Date:_____

Highlights, Quotes, Inspirations, Reflections, Notes...

_____

_____

_____

_____

_____

_____

_____

_____

_____

_____

_____

_____

_____

_____

_____

_____

_____

_____

_____

*"Love, like a river, will cut a new path
whenever it meets an obstacle."*

~Crystal Middlemas

River Log and Details

River (body of water)

_____

Section or run name...

_____

Class ① ② ③ ④ ⑤ +

Vessel (kayak, raft, canoe...)

_____

Shuttle details...

_____
_____

Put-in _____
Take-out _____

Rapids – major & notable (name, features, rating...)

_____
_____
_____
_____
_____
_____

Wildlife and other creatures (bugs, fish, mammals...)

_____
_____
_____
_____

Hikes, points of interest, excursions, fishing spots...

_____
_____
_____
_____
_____

Date _____

Day # _____ of _____ Days

Time on _____ Time off _____

Total time _____

Distance _____

Weather and temp _____

River flow (CFS or feet) _____

Rapids portaged or hazards to avoid...

_____
_____
_____

Who was on the trip...

_____
_____
_____
_____

Campsites & lunch spots (or recommended next visit)..

_____
_____
_____
_____

Favorite food, drink, treat...

_____
_____
_____
_____

✳ Highlights, Quotes, Inspirations, Reflections, Notes...

_____

_____

_____

_____

_____

_____

_____

_____

_____

_____

_____

_____

_____

_____

_____

_____

_____

_____

_____

_____

"Life is a journey. Time is a river.
The door is ajar."

~Jim Butcher

River Log and Details

River (body of water)
_____

Section or run name...
_____

Class ① ② ③ ④ ⑤ +

Vessel (kayak, raft, canoe...)
_____

Shuttle details...
_____
_____

Put-in _____
Take-out _____

Rapids – major & notable (name, features, rating...)
_____
_____
_____
_____
_____

Wildlife and other creatures (bugs, fish, mammals...)
_____
_____
_____
_____

Hikes, points of interest, excursions, fishing spots...
_____
_____
_____
_____

Date _____

Day # _____ of _____ Days

Time on _____ Time off _____

Total time _____

Distance _____

Weather and temp _____

River flow (CFS or feet) _____

Rapids portaged or hazards to avoid...
_____
_____
_____
_____

Who was on the trip...
_____
_____
_____
_____

Campsites & lunch spots (or recommended next visit)...
_____
_____
_____
_____

Favorite food, drink, treat...
_____
_____
_____
_____

Day # _____ of _____ Days: Date:_____

Highlights, Quotes, Inspirations, Reflections, Notes...

_____

_____

_____

_____

_____

_____

_____

_____

_____

_____

_____

_____

_____

_____

_____

_____

_____

_____

"Nature does not hurry,
yet everything is accomplished."

~Lao Tzu

River Log and Details

River (body of water)

_____
Section or run name...

_____

Class ① ② ③ ④ ⑤ +

Vessel (kayak, raft, canoe...)

_____

Shuttle details...

_____
_____

Put-in _____
Take-out _____

Rapids – major & notable
(name, features, rating...)

_____
_____
_____
_____
_____
_____

Wildlife and other creatures
(bugs, fish, mammals...)

_____
_____
_____
_____

Hikes, points of interest,
excursions, fishing spots...

_____
_____
_____
_____
_____

Date _____

Day # _____ of _____ Days

Time on _____ Time off _____

Total time _____

Distance _____
Weather and temp _____

River flow (CFS or feet) _____

Rapids portaged or
hazards to avoid...

_____
_____
_____
_____

Who was on the trip...

_____
_____
_____
_____

Campsites & lunch spots
(or recommended next visit)...

_____
_____
_____
_____

Favorite food, drink, treat...

_____
_____
_____
_____

Highlights, Quotes, Inspirations, Reflections, Notes...

_____

_____

_____

_____

_____

_____

_____

_____

_____

_____

_____

_____

_____

_____

_____

_____

"A river seems a magic thing.
A magic, moving, living part of the very earth itself."
~Laura Gilpin

River Log and Details

River (body of water)

_____

Section or run name...

_____

Class ① ② ③ ④ ⑤ +

Vessel (kayak, raft, canoe...)

_____

Shuttle details...

_____

_____

Put-in _____

Take-out _____

Rapids – major & notable
(name, features, rating...)

_____
_____
_____
_____
_____
_____

Wildlife and other creatures
(bugs, fish, mammals...)

_____
_____
_____
_____

Hikes, points of interest,
excursions, fishing spots...

_____
_____
_____
_____

Date _____

Day # _____ of _____ Days

Time on _____ Time off _____

Total time _____

Distance _____

Weather and temp _____

River flow (CFS or feet) _____

Rapids portaged or
hazards to avoid...

_____
_____
_____
_____

Who was on the trip...

_____
_____
_____
_____

Campsites & lunch spots
(or recommended next visit)...

_____
_____
_____
_____

Favorite food, drink, treat...

_____
_____
_____
_____

Highlights, Quotes, Inspirations, Reflections, Notes...

_____

_____

_____

_____

_____

_____

_____

_____

_____

_____

_____

_____

_____

_____

_____

_____

_____

_____

"The happiest of all lives is a busy solitude."

~Voltaire

River Log and Details

River (body of water)

_____

Section or run name...

_____

Class ① ② ③ ④ ⑤ +

Vessel (kayak, raft, canoe...)

_____

Shuttle details...

_____
_____

Put-in _____
Take-out _____

Rapids – major & notable
(name, features, rating...)

_____
_____
_____
_____
_____
_____

Wildlife and other creatures
(bugs, fish, mammals...)

_____
_____
_____
_____

Hikes, points of interest,
excursions, fishing spots...

_____
_____
_____
_____

Date _____

Day # _____ of _____ Days

Time on _____ Time off _____

Total time _____

Distance _____

Weather and temp _____

River flow (CFS or feet) _____

Rapids portaged or
hazards to avoid...

_____
_____
_____
_____

Who was on the trip...

_____
_____
_____
_____

Campsites & lunch spots
(or recommended next visit)...

_____
_____
_____
_____

Favorite food, drink, treat...

_____
_____
_____
_____

Day # _____ of _____ Days: Date:_____

✴ Highlights, Quotes, Inspirations, Reflections, Notes...

_____

_____

_____

_____

_____

_____

_____

_____

_____

_____

_____

_____

_____

_____

_____

_____

_____

_____

> *"In every walk with nature one receives*
> *far more than he seeks."*
>   ~John Muir

River Log and Details

River (body of water)

_____

Section or run name...

_____

Class ① ② ③ ④ ⑤ +

Vessel (kayak, raft, canoe...)

_____

Shuttle details...

_____
_____

Put-in _____
Take-out _____

Rapids – major & notable
(name, features, rating...)

_____
_____
_____
_____
_____

Wildlife and other creatures
(bugs, fish, mammals...)

_____
_____
_____
_____

Hikes, points of interest,
excursions, fishing spots...

_____
_____
_____
_____

Date _____ 📅

Day # _____ of _____ Days

Time on _____ Time off _____

🕐 Total time _____

Distance _____

Weather and temp _____

River flow (CFS or feet) _____

Rapids portaged or
hazards to avoid...

_____
_____
_____
_____

Who was on the trip...

_____
_____
_____
_____

Campsites & lunch spots
(or recommended next visit)..

_____
_____
_____
_____

Favorite food, drink, treat...

_____
_____
_____
_____

Day # _____ of _____ Days: Date:_____

Highlights, Quotes, Inspirations, Reflections, Notes...

_____

_____

_____

_____

_____

_____

_____

_____

_____

_____

_____

_____

_____

_____

_____

_____

_____

_____

"The river knows the way to the sea: Without a pilot it runs and falls, Blessing all lands with its charity."
~Ralph Waldo Emerson

River Log and Details

River (body of water)

_____
Section or run name...

_____

Class (1) (2) (3) (4) (5) +

Vessel (kayak, raft, canoe...)

_____

Shuttle details...

_____
_____

Put-in _____
Take-out _____

Rapids – major & notable
(name, features, rating...)

_____
_____
_____
_____
_____
_____

Wildlife and other creatures
(bugs, fish, mammals...)

_____
_____
_____
_____

Hikes, points of interest,
excursions, fishing spots...

_____
_____
_____
_____
_____

Date _____

Day # _____ of _____ Days

Time on _____ Time off _____

Total time _____

Distance _____

Weather and temp _____

River flow (CFS or feet) _____

Rapids portaged or
hazards to avoid...

_____
_____
_____
_____

Who was on the trip...

_____
_____
_____
_____

Campsites & lunch spots
(or recommended next visit)..

_____
_____
_____
_____

Favorite food, drink, treat...

_____
_____
_____
_____

Day # _____ of _____ Days: Date:_____

Highlights, Quotes, Inspirations, Reflections, Notes...

_____

_____

_____

_____

_____

_____

_____

_____

_____

_____

_____

_____

_____

_____

_____

_____

_____

_____

_____

_____

_____

"Little by little, one travels far."

~J.R.R. Tolkien

River Log and Details

River (body of water)

_____

Section or run name...

_____

Class ① ② ③ ④ ⑤ +

Vessel (kayak, raft, canoe...)

_____

Shuttle details...

_____
_____

Put-in _____
Take-out _____

Rapids – major & notable
(name, features, rating...)

_____
_____
_____
_____
_____

Wildlife and other creatures
(bugs, fish, mammals...)

_____
_____
_____
_____

Hikes, points of interest,
excursions, fishing spots...

_____
_____
_____
_____

Date _____

Day # _____ of _____ Days

Time on _____ Time off _____

Total time _____

Distance _____

Weather and temp _____

River flow (CFS or feet) _____

Rapids portaged or
hazards to avoid...

_____
_____
_____
_____

Who was on the trip...

_____
_____
_____
_____

Campsites & lunch spots
(or recommended next visit)..

_____
_____
_____
_____

Favorite food, drink, treat...

_____
_____
_____
_____

Highlights, Quotes, Inspirations, Reflections, Notes...

_____

_____

_____

_____

_____

_____

_____

_____

_____

_____

_____

_____

_____

_____

_____

_____

_____

"While the river of life glides along smoothly,
it remains the same river;
only the landscape on either bank seems to change."
~Max Muller

River Log and Details

River (body of water)

_____

Section or run name...

_____

Class ① ② ③ ④ ⑤ +

Vessel (kayak, raft, canoe...)

_____

Shuttle details...

_____
_____

Put-in _____
Take-out _____

Rapids – major & notable
(name, features, rating...)

_____
_____
_____
_____
_____
_____

Wildlife and other creatures
(bugs, fish, mammals...)

_____
_____
_____
_____

Hikes, points of interest,
excursions, fishing spots...

_____
_____
_____
_____
_____

Date _____

Day # _____ of _____ Days

Time on _____ Time off _____

Total time _____

Distance _____

Weather and temp _____

River flow (CFS or feet) _____

Rapids portaged or
hazards to avoid...

_____
_____
_____
_____

Who was on the trip...

_____
_____
_____
_____

Campsites & lunch spots
(or recommended next visit)...

_____
_____
_____
_____

Favorite food, drink, treat...

_____
_____
_____

Day # _____ of _____ Days: Date:_____

Highlights, Quotes, Inspirations, Reflections, Notes...

_____

_____

_____

_____

_____

_____

_____

_____

_____

_____

_____

_____

_____

_____

_____

_____

_____

_____

_____

"Those who contemplate the beauty of the earth find reserves of strength that will endure as long as life lasts."

~Rachel Carson

River Log and Details

River (body of water)

_____

Section or run name...

_____

Class ① ② ③ ④ ⑤ +

Vessel (kayak, raft, canoe...)

_____

Shuttle details...

_____

_____

Put-in _____

Take-out _____

Rapids – major & notable
(name, features, rating...)

_____

_____

_____

_____

_____

_____

Wildlife and other creatures
(bugs, fish, mammals...)

_____

_____

_____

_____

Hikes, points of interest,
excursions, fishing spots...

_____

_____

_____

_____

Date _____

Day # _____ of _____ Days

Time on _____ Time off _____

Total time _____

Distance _____

Weather and temp _____

River flow (CFS or feet) _____

Rapids portaged or
hazards to avoid...

_____

_____

_____

_____

Who was on the trip...

_____

_____

_____

_____

Campsites & lunch spots
(or recommended next visit)..

_____

_____

_____

_____

Favorite food, drink, treat...

_____

_____

_____

_____

Highlights, Quotes, Inspirations, Reflections, Notes...

_____

_____

_____

_____

_____

_____

_____

_____

_____

_____

_____

_____

_____

_____

_____

_____

_____

_____

_____

_____

"If my ship sails from sight, it doesn't mean my journey ends, it simply means the river bends."

~Enoch Powell

River Log and Details

River (body of water)

_____

Section or run name...

_____

Class (1) (2) (3) (4) (5) +

Vessel (kayak, raft, canoe...)

_____

Shuttle details...

_____

_____

Put-in _____

Take-out _____

Rapids – major & notable
(name, features, rating...)

_____

_____

_____

_____

_____

Wildlife and other creatures
(bugs, fish, mammals...)

_____

_____

_____

_____

Hikes, points of interest,
excursions, fishing spots...

_____

_____

_____

_____

_____

Date _____

Day # _____ of _____ Days

Time on _____ Time off _____

Total time _____

Distance _____

Weather and temp _____

River flow (CFS or feet) _____

Rapids portaged or
hazards to avoid...

_____

_____

_____

_____

Who was on the trip...

_____

_____

_____

_____

Campsites & lunch spots
(or recommended next visit)...

_____

_____

_____

_____

Favorite food, drink, treat...

_____

_____

_____

_____

Highlights, Quotes, Inspirations, Reflections, Notes...

_____

_____

_____

_____

_____

_____

_____

_____

_____

_____

_____

_____

_____

_____

_____

_____

_____

_____

_____

"Wherever you go, go with all your heart."

~Confucius

River Log and Details

River (body of water)

_____

Section or run name...

_____

Class ① ② ③ ④ ⑤ +

Vessel (kayak, raft, canoe...)

_____

Shuttle details...

_____

_____

Put-in _____
Take-out _____

Rapids – major & notable
(name, features, rating...)

_____
_____
_____
_____
_____
_____

Wildlife and other creatures
(bugs, fish, mammals...)

_____
_____
_____
_____

Hikes, points of interest,
excursions, fishing spots...

_____
_____
_____
_____

Date _____

Day # _____ of _____ Days

Time on _____ Time off _____

Total time _____

Distance _____

Weather and temp _____

River flow (CFS or feet) _____

Rapids portaged or
hazards to avoid...

_____
_____
_____
_____

Who was on the trip...

_____
_____
_____
_____

Campsites & lunch spots
(or recommended next visit)...

_____
_____
_____
_____

Favorite food, drink, treat...

_____
_____
_____
_____

Day # _____ of _____ Days: Date:_____

✦ Highlights, Quotes, Inspirations, Reflections, Notes...

_____

_____

_____

_____

_____

_____

_____

_____

_____

_____

_____

_____

_____

_____

_____

_____

_____

_____

_____

"There is no rushing a river. When you go there, you go at the pace of the water and that pace ties you into a flow that is older than life on this planet. Acceptance of that pace, even for a day, changes us, reminds us of other rhythms beyond the sound of our own heartbeats."   ~Jeff Rennicke

River Log and Details

River (body of water)

_____

Section or run name...

_____

Class (1) (2) (3) (4) (5) +

Vessel (kayak, raft, canoe...)

_____

Shuttle details...

_____
_____

Put-in _____

Take-out _____

Rapids – major & notable
(name, features, rating...)

_____
_____
_____
_____
_____
_____

Wildlife and other creatures
(bugs, fish, mammals...)

_____
_____
_____
_____

Hikes, points of interest,
excursions, fishing spots...

_____
_____
_____
_____

Date _____

Day # _____ of _____ Days

Time on _____ Time off _____

Total time _____

Distance _____

Weather and temp _____

River flow (CFS or feet) _____

Rapids portaged or
hazards to avoid...

_____
_____
_____
_____

Who was on the trip...

_____
_____
_____
_____

Campsites & lunch spots
(or recommended next visit)...

_____
_____
_____
_____

Favorite food, drink, treat...

_____
_____
_____
_____

Day # _____ of _____ Days: Date:_____

Highlights, Quotes, Inspirations, Reflections, Notes...

_____

_____

_____

_____

_____

_____

_____

_____

_____

_____

_____

_____

_____

_____

_____

_____

_____

_____

"Look deep into nature
and then you will understand everything better."

~Albert Einstein

River Log and Details

River (body of water)

_____

Section or run name...

_____

Class ① ② ③ ④ ⑤ +

Vessel (kayak, raft, canoe...)

_____

Shuttle details...

_____
_____

Put-in _____

Take-out _____

Rapids – major & notable
(name, features, rating...)

_____
_____
_____
_____
_____
_____

Wildlife and other creatures
(bugs, fish, mammals...)

_____
_____
_____
_____

Hikes, points of interest,
excursions, fishing spots...

_____
_____
_____
_____

Date _____

Day # _____ of _____ Days

Time on _____ Time off _____

Total time _____

Distance _____

Weather and temp _____

River flow (CFS or feet) _____

Rapids portaged or
hazards to avoid...

_____
_____
_____
_____

Who was on the trip...

_____
_____
_____
_____

Campsites & lunch spots
(or recommended next visit)...

_____
_____
_____
_____

Favorite food, drink, treat...

_____
_____
_____

Day # _____ of _____ Days: Date:_____

Highlights, Quotes, Inspirations, Reflections, Notes...

_____

_____

_____

_____

_____

_____

_____

_____

_____

_____

_____

_____

_____

_____

_____

_____

_____

"Rivers never go reverse. So try to live like a river,
forget your past and focus on the future."

~Unknown

Favorite Highlights,
Quotes, Inspirations,
Reflections, Notes

_____

_____

_____

_____

_____

_____

_____

_____

_____

Remember the River
And Plan Your
Next Adventure

_____

_____

_____

_____

_____

_____

_____

_____

_____

Made in United States
Troutdale, OR
08/13/2023

12030142R00066